The French Resistance

Resistance

1940-1944

D0723891

Raymond Aubrac

The French Resistance

1940-1944

Translated from French
by Louise Guiney

POCKET 🕮 ARCHIVES

HAZAN

We would like to give special thanks to the Ministère
des Anciens Combattants as well as to the Lyon Centre
d'Histoire de la Résistance for the iconography which
it made available to us.

Cover illustration: The Boussolot (Haute-Loire) post-mistress
receiving a message for transmission to the two maquisards
waiting by the window (Ministère des anciens combattants).

© Éditions Hazan, Paris, 1997
Documentation: Juliette Hazan
Design: Atalante
Production: Anouk Garin
Color separation: Seleoffset, Torino
Printing: Milanostampa, Farigliano

ISBN: 2 85025 567 X
ISSN : 1275-5923
Printed in Italy

Contents

The Development of the French Resistance Movement During the Second World War

The story that follows forms a unique chapter in the history of France. A chapter that opens with a crushing defeat, closes with full participation in a triumphant victory, and passes through incredible shifts of fortune between the two. This is the story of a country overwhelmed by an irresistible power and administered by a servile government in thrall to an occupying army, a country in which patriotic volunteers from all walks of life – many extremely modest – rose in defense of their nation and its ideals. This is the story of how these patriots gradually joined forces to create a single unified movement; and of how, with the aid of their fellow-citizens fighting outside of France, they continued to struggle side-by-side with the allies despite increasingly fierce repression by the enemy. This is the story of the French Resistance Movement during the Second World War.

1940-41 – Resistance Takes Root

The Fall of France - The Franco-German Armistice - The Vichy Government

In June 1940 France suffered one of the most devastating defeats in the nation's history.

When Hitler invaded Poland on the first of September 1939, France and England declared war on Nazi Germany. There followed the frustrating months of "phony war", and a stalemate on either side of the Rhine. Then, suddenly, the Wehrmacht drove a wedge into the Netherlands and Belgium, advancing through the Ardennes. The allied high command was caught off-balance, its front lines battered by the powerful German air and armoured attack. The situation had become hopeless by June 10th, the day Italy entered the war on the German side. However, despite the manifest errors of its leaders, the French army fought bravely in the field, losing nearly 100,000 men in the doomed struggle.

When the invading Germans entered Paris on the 14th of June 1940, millions of panic-stricken French men, women, and children fled southwards. A new French government was formed in Bordeaux, with First World War hero Marshall Pétain named to head it. The following day, Pétain sought an accommodation with the

Germans. On the 25th of June the Franco-German Armistice was officially approved by both sides.

The uprooted people of France were stunned. The armistice split the country in two: the Alsace and Moselle regions were annexed by Germany, the North was occupied by the German army, and the South was governed from the city of Vichy under a regime headed by Marshal Pétain, whose heroism during the First World War still inspired popular confidence. Meanwhile, some two million French prisoners-of-war were shipped to detention camps in Germany.

The conditions specified under the Franco-German armistice were humiliating for France, and immediately aroused defiance in many of the country's citizens. General Charles de Gaulle, who had established a French government-in-exile in London, addressed his compatriots by radio on the 18th of June, calling on both the military and the civilian population to join him and continue the fight. It was also at this point that the prefect of Chartres, one Jean Moulin, attempted suicide rather than obey German orders that he considered dishonourable. But the most effective opposition to the German onslaught came from England which, threatened with a German invasion from the Continent, stood firm behind the stubborn determination of Prime Minister Winston Churchill and the courageous bombing sorties carried out by a handful of Royal Air Force pilots.

The Pétain regime violated principles that had been basic to the French Republic. The motto "Liberty, Equality,

General de Gaulle addressing the nation over the microphones
of the BBC, June 1940.

Fraternity" was replaced by the German-inspired "Work, Family, Country". Only eighty members of the French legislature had had the courage to vote against the proposed new laws; in any case, legislative sessions were soon suspended. Members of the French communist party had already been subject to persecution following the signing of the German-Soviet pact, and additional measures formulated under the Vichy regime now added Jews and Free Masons to the list. The occupying Germans also began to sack French territory for the benefit of the Third Reich. Anti-British propaganda took on new force following the Mers el-Kébir massacre in July, and the handshake exchanged by Pétain and Hitler at Montoire on October 24th sealed Franco-German collaboration.

The Emergence of the Resistance - Movements - Networks

The first stirrings of popular resistance began to be perceptible during the summer and autumn of 1940. Resistance was expressed through isolated gestures – severing telephone lines, sabotaging shipments of goods destined for Germany, assisting escaped prisoners-of-war to flee. In the northern zone, the target was the German army of occupation; in the southern zone, the Vichy regime. Opposition frequently took the form of graffiti painted on public walls or leaflets distributed clandestinely. Newspapers and radio broadcasts were strictly censored in both zones, and people thirsting for reliable information were eager for anything other than the official posters plastering the walls and the strident sloganeering filling the airwaves. This was a tentative period for the organization that was later to become the French Resistance Movement. Operations against the occupying army and the Vichy regime were modest in scope, usually carried out by individuals working alone or in small groups. However, as the four years of German occupation and Vichy government went by, these individuals and small groups increasingly sought each other out in order to unite into larger movements strong enough to play a major role in liberating the country. Yet, even in the early stages, the French Resistance Movement was notable for the creation of underground "networks". After the signing of the Franco-German armistice, these fledgling networks began supplying the British with information about the German armies poised on the opposite side of the Channel. The Free French recruited by General de Gaulle were soon put to work carrying out similar operations. Intelligence had to be gathered, and escapes – especially of allied pilots trying to get back to England – had to be organized. Starting in 1941, sabotage was added to resistance operations. Methods varied, and means were often primitive. For example, in the beginning at least, the radio equipment used by resistance networks for communications was heavy, bulky, and difficult to conceal.

The men and women active in these movements and networks laboured under difficult conditions. They often led double lives, and they had to make up the rules of the game as they went along. They ran the risk of betrayal every time they recruited new members for underground work; and, lastly, all the money for equipment, expenses, lodging, and travel came out of their own pockets or those of their friends.

As the Resistance Movement grew, so too did official repression. The Vichy government continued the persecution of communists begun at the end of 1939, and gradually extended it to anyone found distributing clandestine leaflets or newspapers. In the northern zone, the German police acted in conjunction with the French police to quell opposition by keeping the populace under a tight and punitive rein. In December 1940 an engineer named Bonsergent was shot for jostling a German non-commissioned officer in the street. In 1941 the Honoré d'Estienne d'Orves intelligence network was destroyed. The Musée de l'Homme network was later decimated after being betrayed by one of its members, and the official posters on public walls began to report increasing numbers of arrests and executions.

However, despite every obstacle placed in its path, the incipient Resistance Movement proved that patriotism and love of freedom had not disappeared from France. On November 11th 1940, university and lycée students gathered on the Champs Elysées, some of them carrying two fishing poles (in French, *deux gaules* or *de Gaulle*). In early 1941 a British radio broadcast called on the French to paint "V for Victory" signs in public places,

Boris Vildé, founder of the Musée d'Homme network, one of the earliest
in the Resistance Movement. Following the betrayal of this network by an informer,
Vildé and many other members were executed in February 1942
by the Germans at Mont-Valérien.

and this was done in many French cities. In May 1941 the miners of the Nord and Pas de Calais regions organized a general strike. But after each such incident, German repression doubled in intensity.

The Expansion of the War - First Sabotage Attacks
Until June of 1941, England and the isolated resistance groups working inside France stood alone in their struggle against nazi Germany and fascist Italy. But the year 1941 was to see the war expand to virtually the entire world. Hitler invaded the USSR on the 21st of June, and in December came the Japanese attack on Pearl Harbor that brought the United States into the conflict. From the time of the German-Soviet pact until that year, the French communist party – despite the fact that many of its militant members had joined the ranks of the Resistance Movement – maintained an ambivalent attitude towards the war. But now it reacted vigorously, actively participating in the support and organization of the early armed phase of the opposition struggle. Colonel Fabien led an operation in Paris, and there were bombings in Nantes and Bordeaux. But each new incident was followed by massive executions of hostages held by the Germans.
It was during this period of escalation that a major breach developed in the Resistance Movement and among its leaders in London and France. One divisive question was whether or not the Resistance should attack German soldiers directly. De Gaulle and his military

advisors recommended restraint for the time being, but numerous politicians and even the British government held the opposite view. A corollary to this question was whether the Resistance Movement based in France should devote all of its efforts to preparing for the allied invasion, or engage in "immediate action". German repression increased in response to every new Resistance initiative, with Vichy minister of the interior Pucheu even going so far as to participate personally in selecting the communist and Jewish hostages shot at Chateaubriand. But the intensification of German and Vichy repression served only to stiffen the resolve of the men and women in the Resistance Movement.

1942 – Resistance becomes Organized

The Clandestine Press

In 1942 the French Resistance Movement achieved formal organization and began to spread dramatically. This was also the year when communications were established with London – an important point.

Resistance groups often concentrated their efforts on the publication and distribution of opposition newspapers. The underground press was active in the North and even more so in the South, where (until the zone was occupied in November 1942) it was easier to operate with impunity. Even under the best of circumstances underground journalism was a complex and high-risk venture, but the rewards were great. The clandestine press

Henri Frenay, founder and leader of the resistance network affiliated with the clandestine newspaper *Combat*.

stimulated recruitment to the resistance cause, and slaked
the thirst for information on the part of a public grow-
ing more and more aware of the true physical and moral
nature of the occupation and the progress of the war.
Putting out a clandestine newspaper naturally involved
writing copy, but this was the easy part. Talented writ-
ers were in generous supply; reliable news could be gathered from BBC broadcasts and programmes beamed
from neutral countries; and news analysis and editorial
comment simply reflected the political line of the group
putting out the paper. The hardest part of the task was
to locate a printing press. Cooperative printers ran terrible personal risks, and many paid for their altruism
with their freedom or their lives. It was also difficult to
obtain paper, which had to be extracted from shipments
to presses working for official newspaper and book pub-
lishers. Distribution, lastly, required transport, generally by rail and under heavy camouflage. Personal
delivery then had to be made to the object of the entire
operation – the reader. Sometimes different networks
distributing different newspapers used a single contact
who re-directed each publication, depending on its
slant, to the appropriate reader. These newspaper-dis-
tribution networks formed the core of France's various
resistance groups.
Prominent among dozens of Resistance titles were
Libération-Nord and Défense de la France in the North;
and Combat, Franc-Tireur, and Libération-Sud in the
South. These newspapers shared their names with France's

Jean-Pierre Lévy, a leader of the resistance network affiliated with
the clandestine newspaper *Le Franc-Tireur*.

Emmanuel d'Astier de la Vigerie, founder and leader of the *Libération-Sud* newspaper and resistance movement.

major resistance networks. The French communist party also published l'Humanité, l'Avant-Garde, and various other newspapers for specialised readerships, such as l'Université Libre. The National Front, a broad-based movement created under the aegis of the communist party, also distributed its own clandestine publications. Although the Resistance Movement as a whole was gradually consolidated, the original groups clung to their own newspapers and distribution networks. Careful study by historians of the these newspapers' content has revealed policy differences among them, but the basic message was the same: opposition to the occupying Nazi army and to French collaborators, opposition to the Vichy government (although this was tentative at first), and glorification of the victories won by the Resistance and the allied armies.

Jean Moulin – Progress Towards Unification

As noted above, 1942 was the year that consolidation of the Resistance Movement into a single unit began. Unification was masterminded by the former Chartres prefect Jean Moulin, known as "Rex" or "Max", who had attempted suicide rather than face dishonour, and was subsequently removed from office by the Vichy government. Moulin began his career as an opposition figure by gathering documentary information on fledgling resistance groups. He took the fruits of his research to London, and returned in early January 1942 with orders from General de Gaulle to enlist all resistance movements in the liberation cause, to coordinate the movements in the southern zone, and to mold paramilitary divisions into an underground army. In 1941, de Gaulle had concentrated his efforts on organizing the Free French Liberation Forces (F.F.L.) and their networks outside of France; and, indeed, these dedicated groups ultimately fought side-by-side with the allies in every theatre of operations. But by 1942 he had come to understand the key role played by the resistance movements working inside France itself.

Jean Moulin distributed funds allocated in London to the resistance networks in France, and he also supervised air operations and transport. He created the first unified resistance divisions, the B.I.P. (Bureau d'Information et de Presse) and C.G.E. (Comité Général d'Études). The Comité de Coordination des Mouvements Unis de Résistance (M.U.R.) was founded in the autumn of 1942, as was the Armée Secrète commanded by General Delestraint. By this time Christian Pineau had obtained a formal undertaking from General de Gaulle supporting democracy and republican institutions. Resistance movements in the southern zone were assigned officers through whom they could communicate with London via the B.C.R.A. (Bureau Central de Renseignements et d'Action).

The increasing power of the Resistance Movement once again gave rise to fresh repression on the part of the Nazis. Under the Oberg-Bouquet agreements, the Vichy police were ordered to work in "cooperation" with the

German police, although the French were actually subordinate to the Germans. The summer of 1942 saw the first massive round-ups of both expatriate and native-French Jews and, in response, the formation of the first local humanitarian efforts responsible for saving so many children from death. Furthermore, although the Catholic hierarchy had been unstinting in its support of the Vichy regime, a few individual prelates now began to speak out against the anti-Semitic persecutions.

The Turning-Point in the War

During the winter of 1942-43 the balance on the battlefield shifted. The November allied landing in North Africa marked the beginning of the re-conquest of Europe. The Wehrmacht, in violation of the Franco-German armistice, reacted by invading the southern zone of France, confiscating the weapons of the French "Armistice Army", forcing the Vichy government to hand over all the weapons stockpiled by the French high command in 1940, and sinking the French fleet lying off Toulon. Most significant of all, however, was the fact that Marshal Pétain refused to leave France and join the French forces in Algiers, thus confirming his policy of collaboration with the enemy – a rude shock to many who had given him their loyal and sincere support. Meanwhile, the battle of Stalingrad in the USSR put an end to the German advance on the eastern front. The surrender of the Von Paulus army during the first weeks of 1943 was a solemn harbinger of Soviet victories to come.

When the Armistice Army was disbanded, hundreds of its commissioned and non-commissioned officers joined the Resistance, either through existing networks, or through the newly formed O.R.A. (Organisation de Résistance de l'Armée). By now the Germans were suffering badly from lack of man-power on the home front, caused by the insatiable demands of their army and the dearth of volunteers to fill the gap. In February 1943 they ordered the Vichy government to form the S.T.O. (Service du Travail Obligatoire), which drafted three categories of young French men aged 21 to 23 years into forced labour. The men involved were naturally reluctant to leave for Germany, and many sought exemption on medical grounds, or went into hiding with friends and relatives. Some hid out in forests and mountains, giving rise to the term *Maquis* (French for *woods*) to designate a new underground movement that was to receive ready assistance from both the civilian population and the organized Resistance Movement.

1943 – The Resistance Comes of Age

The Maquis – False Identification Papers – Mutual Support

The Maquis faced problems of food, shelter, lines of command, and – for the many eager volunteers seeking to participate in active warfare against the occupying forces – weapons. Food and shelter were supplied mainly by the civilian population, sometimes in return for financial remuneration from the Resistance. Lines of command were established by the Armée Secrète and former members of the Armistice Army. The thorniest problem, largely unsolved until the spring of 1944, was weaponry. With few exceptions – notably for the groups serving in Savoy under Commandant Valette and in the Toulouse region under Captain Pommies – French weapons had all been either destroyed or consigned to the Germans and Italians.

A major concern during 1943 was the organization of the Maquis. By the end of the year, tens of thousands of young men had opted for civil disobedience, and the Resistance found itself with new problems to solve.

These young men needed counterfeit identification papers in order to elude capture by local and national police. They needed other documents as well: food-rationing cards and coupons and, depending on their age, army discharge and work papers. A number of identification-paper counterfeiting centres were therefore created in order to meet the demand. This task involved mobilizing printing presses, graphic artists, and – often – registry-office clerks in town halls.

Another sector of activity, mutual assistance, was also developed during this period. Every resistance movement and network organized its own mutual-assistance branch to help the families of the men and women who had fallen victim to oppression, and to tend the ill and – especially – the wounded. Hundreds of physicians in country and city alike contributed their skills to the cause. Meanwhile, escape routes to Switzerland and Spain were opened for fleeing resistance fighters and persecuted Jews.

Unification - the C.N.R.

The year 1943 also marked the complete unification of the Resistance Movement. Early that year Jean Moulin, accompanied by General Delestraint, left France on a mission to London. He returned with an expanded mandate covering not just the southern zone, as before, but the entire country. His efforts were directed towards a dual goal: organizing a unified Resistance Movement; and strengthening the influence and authority of General de Gaulle. His task was made particularly difficult by the great diversity of the individual resistance movements. In 1942-43 there were three main categories: the "Gaullist" groups, which in the southern zone had already joined to form the M.U.R.; the National Front groups, directed by the restructured communist party; and the military groups (usually "Giraudist" and anti-communist) that with the dissolution of the Armistice Army congregated in the O.R.A. If each of these groups had gone their own way, replicating France's prewar political sectarianism, the Resistance Movement would have remained totally ineffective. This danger was underscored by the fact that members of the French high command in London also sometimes split along political lines, which resulted (to take just one example) in the strict limitations placed on equipment supplied early in the war to resistance groups inside France and later to the Maquis, which was suspected of communist leanings.

The engines of unity were a shared objective – to vanquish the occupying army and its Vichy puppets – and the political skills of London's deputy, Jean Moulin. However, this great "unifier" had first to resolve another problem: the stubborn independence of the resistance leaders inside France. One crisis was particularly difficult to handle. This was the "Swiss Case" involving combat chief Henri Frenay, who unilaterally attempted to obtain financial aid from the United States and thus to gain a measure of independence from the French high command in London.

In order to mold these disparate and sometimes wayward groups into a coherent whole, General de Gaulle and Jean Moulin formed the National Resistance Council (C.N.R.), made up of representatives from all the resistance movements, from the labour unions, from those political parties (communist and socialist) considered "resistant" in spirit, and also from some of the more moderate political factions. Although the creation of the C.N.R. was instrumental in alleviating the doubts continually expressed by U.S. president Roosevelt, who suspected de Gaulle of being undemocratic, many of the resistance leaders themselves were less than eager to accept it. The members of the Resistance Movement were all patriots. They were also volunteers committed to civil disobedience against the collaborationist Vichy

The C.N.R. *From left to right*: Debu-Bridel (Fédération Républicaine),
Villon (Front National), Tessier (C.F.T.C.), Chambeirou (secretary),
Copeau (*Libération-Sud*), Laniel (Alliance Démocratique),

Lecompte-Boinet (C.D.L.R.), Bidault (Christian-Democrat), Mutter (C.D.L.L.), Ribière (*Libération-Nord*), Lévy (*Le Franc-Tireur*), Mayer (S.F.I.O.), Bastid (Radical), Gillot (French Communist Party), Meunier (secretary), Saillant (C.G.T.).

government. Their dream was to restore the French
republic and its ideals. They had analysed the reasons
behind the defeat of France by the Germans; they under-
stood the cowardice and perfidy of the "elitist" political class; they sought increased social justice; and they
feared a return to the old pre-war political parties.

Jean Moulin himself presided over the first meeting of
the C.N.R., held in Paris on the 27th of May 1943.
Despite the many difficulties involved, the new organization scored an immediate success that went far
beyond merely convincing the allied powers of its cred-
ibility. The Council stood behind General de Gaulle in
the "de Gaulle-Giraud" conflict, helping the general to
prevail over Giraud, who had been supported by the
U.S.A. The Council also served as a powerful catalyst for
national unity on the eve of decisive events for which
it crafted an appropriate strategy; and it paved the way
for the future of a France destined once again to become
free and independent. The C.N.R. program, including
the article dealing with preparations for the Liberation,
laid down the main guidelines for the social and eco-
nomic policies implemented during the first months
following the Liberation.

Repression – Intelligence – the C.F.L.N.
In 1943 the Resistance Movement continued to gain in
strength, and German repression continued to inten-
sify. Early in the year the Vichy government formed a
Militia under the leadership of Joseph Darnand, who

recruited a mixed bag of adventurers and fanatic collaborationists for this new arm of repression and persecution designed to reinforce the work of the regular French police force and the German Gestapo.

On the 9th of June General Delestraint was arrested in Paris. On the 21st, in Caluire, a suburb of Lyon, Jean Moulin was taken by the Gestapo. He, along with key members of his military command, had been denounced to the authorities by a traitor in their midst. When members of the French Resistance were arrested, they were first tortured, and then either sent before a firing squad or deported to die a lingering death in German concentration camps. Moulin was tortured by the infamous Klaus Barbie and died during his transfer to Germany. But he never once revealed any of the secrets in his safekeeping. Here was a man who amply deserved his emblematic position as the leader of French resistance to enemy occupation. Moulin had begun his career as a dedicated public servant of the French Republic, and he continued to fulfill this mission until the day of his death.

Despite the dangers and risks, the Resistance had by this time become indestructible. Jean Moulin – who had served as General de Gaulle's deputy, as a member of the French Commission in London, and also as president of the C.N.R. – was replaced by two men: Claude Bouchinet-Serreules, as interim deputy; and Georges Bidault, as president of the C.N.R. General Delestraint was replaced by Colonel Dejussieu-Pontcarral, but because the day-to-day command of the Armée Secrète was decentralised, it was several months before his appointment became official. By the end of 1943 the resistance intelligence networks had attained a remarkable level of effectiveness. Radio communications were facilitated by modern equipment, but radio operators continued to pay a high price for their work, which the Germans were able to pinpoint using radio-wave direction finders. Nevertheless, information on Wehrmacht defenses and troop movements was communicated with increasing speed to the allied high command.

Underground newspapers were being distributed within France at the rate of some two million copies per month, the C.N.R. and its various commissions were active, and General de Gaulle's deputies maintained communications between London and Algiers, where the General himself – having prevailed decisively over General Giraud – headed the French Commission of National Liberation (C.F.L.N.).

The greatest weakness of the Resistance Movement was lack of weapons. These were provided only sporadically by an allied high command apparently reluctant to arm civilians. Although weapon-drops by parachute became more frequent as the date for the allied invasion neared, generally only small arms were delivered.

At the end of 1943 a meeting of the Provisional Advisory Assembly was convened in Algiers. The assembly included representatives from the Resistance Movement, former French legislators, and other key figures. As with the C.N.R., though to a lesser degree, the membership of this assembly was contested by many in the Resistance Movement.

In September 1943 the Corsican Resistance Movement staged a revolt, and with the assistance of the French forces based in Algiers successfully liberated the island.

1944 – The Liberation

Preparations for the Liberation

The French government-in-exile in Algiers, led by Commissioner of the Interior Emmanuel d'Astier, founder of the resistance newspaper Libération-Sud, now began to make preparations for the measures to be implemented after the Liberation. In carrying out this task, advice was sought from the Advisory Assembly (on women's suffrage, for example) and from the C.G.E., a commission of experts working inside France. During these tense months of high hope and political manoeuvering, the government's proposals were submitted to all Resistance organizations for approval.

At the beginning of June 1944, the BBC began broadcasting coded messages signaling the Resistance to begin major sabotage of the enemy. On the 6th of June, following a decision by the allied high command, two hundred messages triggered "D-Day" sabotage operations and generalised guerrilla warfare. The goal was to impede German troop movements directed against consolidation of the allied beachhead. The complete success of the Resistance in carrying out this mission impressed the allied high command, which immediately began supplying all the weapons requested and parachuting liaison personnel (the Jedburgh missions) into France.

Several French cities (Annonay, Nantua, Guéret, Tulle) were liberated, only to be retaken by the enemy. The reason for this was the increased vulnerability of land and air operations that, although they impeded the enemy, were now being carried out in the open.

General Koenig, recently named commander-in-chief of the F.F.I. (Forces Françaises de l'Intérieur), attempted to limit the scope of operations exposing enthusiastic but poorly armed members of the Resistance to enemy fire. However, final decisions depended on the judgement of local resistance leaders.

Mobilisation of the Maquis – and Reprisals

Thousands of volunteers responded to the June 6th call by flocking to *mobilisateurs*, or Maquis staging areas. However, the policy of selecting specific areas from which to launch offensive actions immediately rendered them vulnerable to enemy attack. The only way to secure the areas effectively would have been to supply them with heavy weapons and synchronise their operations with the allied landings. This proved impossible for a variety of reasons, and conflicts such as the battle of Mont Mouchet in the Massif Central region exacted heavy losses from the Maquis and local civilians.

With assistance from the Wehrmacht, the Vichy government's forces of internal repression eliminated a major Maquis centre in Savoy, where the battles of Glières was fought in February and March. The Maquis operation in the Vercors – which took place between the Normandy and Provence landings – involved 20,000 German fighting-men, including 500 SS troops landed on the plateau by glider. Maquisards and civilians alike were massacred by the enemy. No one was spared, not even the wounded and the physicians attending them. This blood-bath left a terrible memory etched in the minds of those who survived it.

The Resistance and the Liberation of France

During the battles of Normandy and Brittany, the F.F.I. and the underground intelligence networks provided the allied armies with precious support by harassing the enemy and reporting troop movements to the allied high command. Following the Normandy landings and invasion in early August, the F.F.I. joined the allied offensive, helped cut off enemy garrisons, and laid siege to "pockets" along the Atlantic coast (St. Nazaire, Lorient, Royan). Throughout the rest of France, mobile guerrilla units sabotaged communications, attacked convoys, hampered enemy troop movements, and sometimes liberated major areas completely.

Immediately after the allied landing in Provence on the 15th of August, the resistance forces joined the conflict, opening the Alpine route over which the allied armies were able to reach Grenoble on the 22nd of August. On the 21st of August the F.F.I. triggered the insurrection of Marseille, and General de Lattre de Tassigny's African troops entered the city on the 23rd of August. When the German garrison surrendered on the 28th, the allied armies continued their advance through the Rhône valley.

In Paris, after several days of general strikes, insurrection broke out on the 19th of August. The F.F.I. erected barricades from which they fought for control of the city, clearing the way for the entrance of General Leclerc's 2nd Armoured Division on the 24th. On the 25th of August the German garrison surrendered, and General de Gaulle made his triumphal march down the Champs Elysées in a liberated Paris.

Meanwhile, the allies fought fierce battles as they advanced inland (north of the Loire; in Provence and the Rhône valley) from their two landing sites before joining forces in the Vosges and Alsace and crossing the Rhine. In many parts of France during this period, members of the Resistance fought on alone against the Germans, harassing the enemy, restricting troop movements, taking prisoners-of-war, and liberating numerous areas. These campaigns resulted, notably, in the liberation of Limoges, Brive, Castres, and (after heavy fighting) the Toulouse region. Also to the credit of the French Resistance Movement was the surrender of the Elster Battalion and the flight from Bordeaux of 20,000 enemy soldiers, later captured by the Auvergne F.F.I.

After the August landings in Provence, General de Lattre de Tassigny offered to incorporate the F.F.I. volunteers into his army. This "amalgam" involving over 100,000 men was not easy to accomplish, and it created a host of material and psychological problems. Additional equipment had to be obtained from the U.S. forces, and conflicting attitudes among the French reconciled.

However, the consolidated French force was able to render valuable service in mid-September, when the allied advance was halted by a German line of defense extending from the North Sea to the Vosges. Later, as winter fighting in a harsh climate began, the relief provided to the French troops from Africa by their F.F.I. compatriots was doubly welcome. The F.F.I. also distinguished itself on the Alpine front during this phase of the liberation struggle.

* * *

The French Resistance Movement was rooted, first, in popular opposition to the armistice with Germany. Those who opposed the armistice found themselves severed from those who – sometimes with unconcealed joy – embraced it. And, although Marshal Pétain's heroism during the First World War had earned him universal respect in France, his prominent role in the French high command's lack of preparation for the 1939 German invasion could not easily be forgotten or forgiven.

When General de Gaulle chose to follow a course of patriotic insubordination, establishing a government-in-exile in London and calling on the men and women of France to join him, many were eager to do so. Young and old alike expressed their support in words and actions, insignificant as the latter may have seemed against the combined forces of the German Wehrmacht and the Vichy regime. But the French determination to resist oppression was manifest.

England's courageous fight against invasion encouraged members of the French Resistance operating both inside and outside their country. In an occupied France deprived of every civil liberty, the small groups that were later to form the major Resistance networks began to emerge.

These people came from all walks of life and represented every hue in the political spectrum. But they reconciled their differences in the interest of unity, an imperative if their common cause were to be successful. Although historians have tended to scrutinise and underscore the "conflicts" within the Resistance Movement, they would be better advised to train their sights on the unity hewn from a situation rife with obstacles to concerted action. From 1942 onwards, the spectre of a divided country loomed – a spectre that became reality in other countries with active wartime resistance movements such as Poland, Yugoslavia, and Greece.

An unbridgeable gulf could also have opened up between the French high command in London and an internal resistance movement grievously lacking in equipment – especially weapons – with which to combat repression that grew more cruel with every passing year.

The achievements of Jean Moulin, working under orders from General de Gaulle – who was well aware of his debt to the Resistance – were instrumental in keeping this dual risk at bay. The creation of the C.N.R. and its cooperation with deputies sent to France, first by the London and later the Algerian Commission, reflected the success of this two-pronged effort. Jean Moulin paid for his accomplishment with his life, but he fulfilled his mission.

Thanks to the sacrifices made by tens of thousands of French patriots who were tortured, shot, or deported and left to die in concentration camps; and thanks to the courage of the workers, peasants, intellectuals, soldiers, and foreign militants who joined the battle for freedom and independence, France was able to play a major role in the allied victory and regain its former rank in the community of nations.

Sealed in blood, the unity of the Resistance Movement made it possible for France to participate actively in the struggle for liberation, and to earn full recognition for this participation from the country's allies. And it was this unity that also enabled Charles de Gaulle to gather up the reins of government and restore democratic freedoms to France.

The Resistance Movement fought for, and won, the return of freedom to France. If today this freedom is abused by some, including those who exploit it in order to undermine it, that is perhaps because freedom's message is a difficult one to transmit.

The Occupation

"V" for Victory sign and banner proclaiming "Germany will win on all fronts"
on the Eiffel Tower. Paris, July 1941.
Opposite page: German troops marching down the Champs-Elysées.

Vichy regime propaganda poster.

Food becomes scarce.

Jews captured during the May 15th (1941) round-up preparing to board trains
at the Austerlitz railway terminal that will take them to camps in Pithiviers
and Beaune-la-Rolande.

German posters announcing the anti-Semitic measures implemented in the Northern Zone.

The Lamarck metro station being used as a bomb shelter.

Occupation

A pedicab in the snow, Place de l'Opéra (Paris), 1942.
Following page: Crossing the demarcation line at Moulins.

Démarka[tion]
Ligne de [...]
Überschre[iten]
Passage

Propaganda, Counterfeit
Identity Papers

A poster of Marshal Pétain affixed to the columns of an elevated metro line,
on which patriots have drawn the "V" for Victory sign.

Resistance graffiti on a German propaganda poster.

Handwritten flyer encouraging students to join the 11 November 1940 demonstration at the Arc de Triomphe.

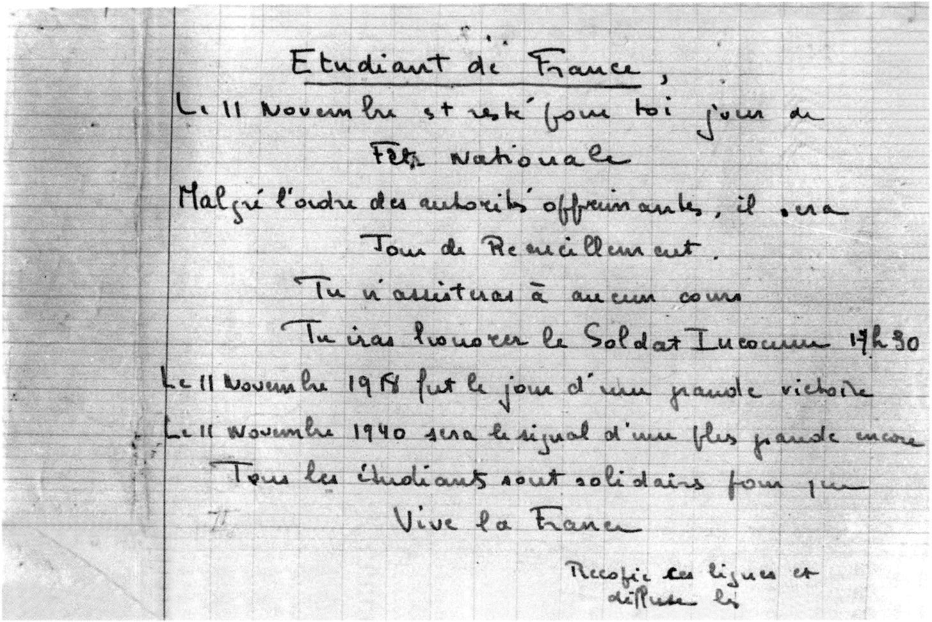

Étudiant de France,

Le 11 novembre est resté pour toi jour de
Fête nationale

Malgré l'ordre des autorités oppressantes, il sera
Jour du Recueillement

Tu n'assisteras à aucun cours

Tu iras honorer le Soldat Inconnu 17h.30

Le 11 novembre 1918 fut le jour d'une grande victoire

Le 11 novembre 1940 sera le signal d'une plus grande encore

Tous les étudiants sont solidaires pour un
Vive la France

Recopie ce ligne et
diffuse

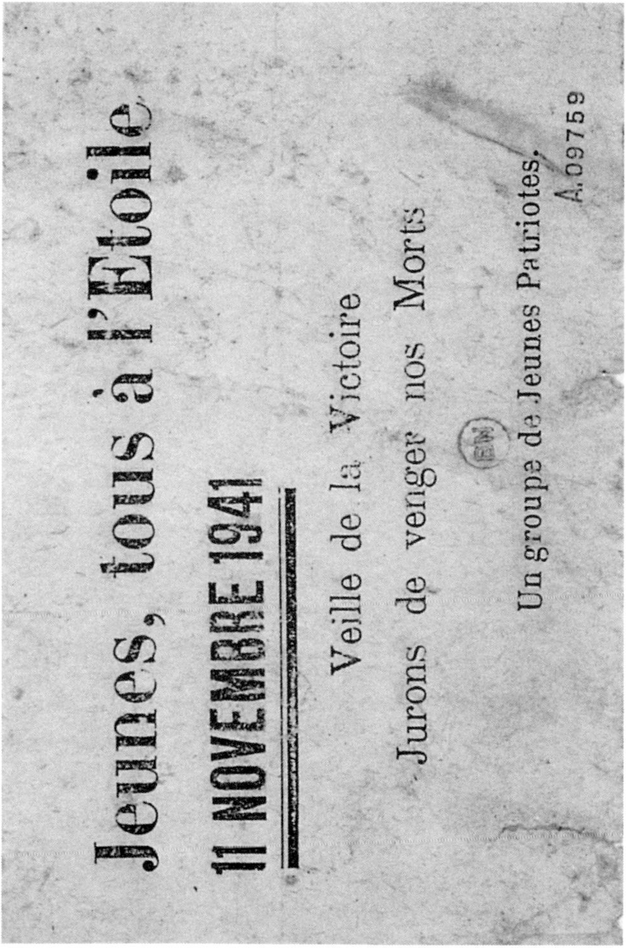

Jeunes, tous à l'Etoile

11 NOVEMBRE 1941

Veille de la Victoire

Jurons de venger nos Morts.

Un groupe de Jeunes Patriotes.

A.09759

Resistance leaflet, 1941.

Resistance leaflet supporting De Gaulle.

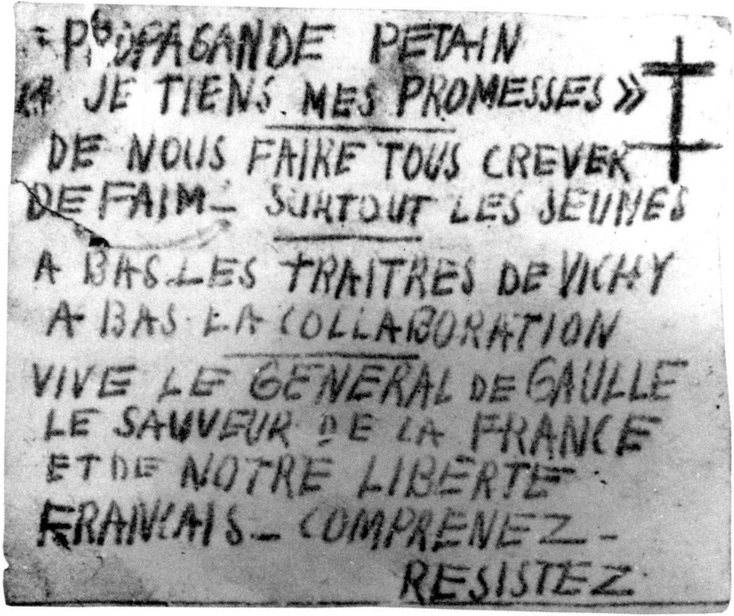

« PROPAGANDE PÉTAIN
« JE TIENS MES PROMESSES »

DE NOUS FAIRE TOUS CREVER
DE FAIM — SURTOUT LES JEUNES

A BAS LES TRAITRES DE VICHY
A BAS LA COLLABORATION

VIVE LE GÉNÉRAL DE GAULLE
LE SAUVEUR DE LA FRANCE
ET DE NOTRE LIBERTÉ
FRANÇAIS — COMPRENEZ —
RESISTEZ

A leaflet, apparently of Alsatian origin, on which the two dots in front of the cock's beak probably represent the cities of Strasbourg and Colmar.

Handbill designed to be glued on the "Red List" (see p.181).
Opposite page: Cyclist distributing leaflets in Paris.

Clandestine printing press in Paris.

The method used to generate power for printing counterfeit identification papers during power cut-offs.

Clandestine printing press. The crate was used to camouflage the press.

The clandestine newspapers published by the three major Resistance networks:
Le Franc-Tireur, *Libération*, and *Combat*.

92

l'Université libre

RIOM, RIOM,.....
Rira bien qui rira
le dernier....

nº 50 MARS 1942

Georges Politzer & Jacques Solomon

Ont été arrêtés et livrés aux Allemands par la police de Pucheu.
Unis à tous les patriotes, engageons le Combat pour arracher
des prisons ceux qui sont la gloire de la pensée française.

SAUVONS LES!

Malgré les odieuses brimades qu'elle a subies depuis l'occupation nazie de la France, malgré les arrestations arbitraires et les violences, malgré les condamnations d'un grand nombre de ses membres, l'Université résiste fermement à l'oppresseur.

Après avoir détenu arbitrairement pendant de longues semaines les plus grands savants français vivants, les Professeurs BOREL, LANGEVIN, LAPICQUE, MAUGUIN et COTTON, les nazis ont dû céder devant la volonté de l'Université de Paris de défendre l'Intelligence française.

C'est pourquoi la rage des hitlériens et de leurs laquais de Vichy est grande. Ils veulent de nouveau frapper de grands coups pour briser la résistance et l'unité de l'Université.

C'est ainsi que nous venons d'apprendre de nouvelles arrestations d'Intellectuels parmi lesquels Georges POLITZER, Agrégé de l'Université et Jacques SOLOMON, Docteur ès Sciences, bien connus de tous comme d'ardents patriotes.

De plus, nous sommes sans nouvelles du Professeur Paul LANGEVIN qui était en résidence surveillée à Troyes. Le bruit court que Paul LANGEVIN aurait de nouveau -pour la 3ème fois- été arrêté.

Nous lançons un cri d'alarme. L'Université ne laissera pas accomplir de nouveaux crimes. Nous ne voulons pas que se renouvellent les tortures dont ont été victimes Fernand HOLWECK et les nombreux intellectuels arrêtés, torturés ou fusillés par von STULPNAGEL.

L'indignation grandit dans l'Université.

Non, l'Université ne laissera pas arrêter et assassiner ses meilleurs représentants. Non, l'Université ne laissera pas les bourreaux augmenter la trop longue série de leurs crimes.

POLITZER et SOLOMON sont en danger !

Universitaires français, savants professeurs, chercheurs, instituteurs étudiants, envoyez votre protestation au Recteur, aux Doyens des Facultés. Obligez-les à agir pour sauver de la mort de nouvelles victimes.

Unissons-nous dans nos comités de FRONT NATIONAL pour l'Indépendance de notre pays.

Engageons le combat aux côtés de tous les patriotes français pour obtenir par tous les moyens la libération des nôtres.

Rien n'arrêtera la volonté de l'Université de lutter jusqu'au bout pour la liberté et l'indépendance de la France.

l'Université libre.

L'Université Libre, newspaper published by the academic arm of the Front National.

fime seulement est publiée par la presse contrôlée), des actes de sabotage et des attentats commis sur le territoire métropolitain pendant la période qui va du 15 juillet au 15 août 1943. Ce palmarès de la résistance française se suffit à lui-même. Il montre que les patriotes de France ne sont ni moins courageux ni moins entreprenants que leurs frères de Hollande, de Yougoslavie, du Danemark, de Grèce ou de Pologne.

Le 5 septembre à Vichy Laval a convoqué le ministre de la Justice, le Chef de la gendarmerie et plusieurs spécialistes de la police. L'entrevue, fut consacrée, déclarait le communiqué officiel, à l'examen des questions intéressant la sécurité du territoire. Nous n'en doutons pas un instant...

LES MOUVEMENTS UNIS DE RÉSISTANCE

COMMUNIQUÉ DES GROUPES FRANCS DES M.U.R.

18 juillet — La voie est coupée au poste kilométrique 389 en face de l'usine Gnome et Rhône ; rupture d'un rail sur 40 cm. Trafic interrompu pendant 2 heures sur la voie montante de Toulouse à Paris.

19 juillet — La voie est coupée sur la ligne Nimes-Lyon à l'Ardoise et Roquelaure. Arrêt du trafic pendant 9 heures.

20 juillet — Au P.K. 495 explosion au passage du G.B. à 4h.59 Rupture d'un rail et déraillement du fourgon et de trois voitures. Retard de 4 heures dans la marche des trains. Le trafic normal n'a pu reprendre que le troisième jour.

24 juillet — Le vérin hydraulique du dépôt de la gare de Clermont est attaqué par un groupe franc. Le vérin et deux compresseurs sautent. Les machines endommagées doivent être transportées à Lyon pour réparations. Toute l'activité du dépôt est arrêtée. Plusieurs millions de dégâts.

27 juillet — La voie est coupée entre Oullins et Lyon et le trafic doit être détourné par Chasse. La même nuit une autre équipe coupe la voie aux environs de Meursault dans la Côte d'Or : un train allemands déraille.

30 juillet — Dans la nuit du 30 au 31 un G.F. fait dérailler un train allemand à Fontaine Saint Marcel entre Châlons et Chagny. Une centaine de soldats allemands sont tués.

31 juillet — Aux ateliers Maritain la rotative est entièrement détruite. Plusieurs millions de dégâts

1 Août — Attaques de quatre wagons de produits chimiques qui sont détruits.

Marseille 7 août — La nuit dernière un train de munitions allemand a sauté entre St-Raphaël et Marseille. Dégâts importants. Les trains ont subi des retards considérables.

Chambéry 7 août — On signale plusieurs attentats durant les derniers jours en Savoie. Le 7 août les rails ont été déboulonnés dans le tunnel du Paradis entre Culoz et Bellegarde. Un train de marchandises a déraillé et le trafic vers la Suisse par Genève-Cornavin a été arrêté. Le trafic par le viaduc de Longaray a été également interrompu.

Report on resistance fighters published in *Libération-Sud*, 15 September 1943.

Consignes aux Militants

A mesure que s'étend notre action, votre responsabilité de militant grandit. L'heure de la libération approche, et votre rôle devient de plus en plus important. De plus en plus difficile aussi. Vous êtes à l'avant-garde du combat. Vous êtes de plus en plus visés par la police de Hitler-Laval. Votre devoir est de poursuivre la lutte. Vous ne conserverez la liberté d'action, vous n'éviterez l'arrestation de vos amis que si vous méditez et appliquez scrupuleusement les consignes suivantes :

1) Ne bavardez jamais, pas de paroles inutiles.

2) Ne citez jamais vos amis par leur nom. Utilisez des pseudonymes, pas de prénoms.

3) Ne téléphonez pas : écrivez le moins possible : la censure ouvre 30 % des lettres.

4) Jamais de listes de noms ou d'adresses.

5) Jamais de réunions de plus de quatre amis, sans précautions très grandes.

6) Utilisez la poste pour la diffusion. C'est un excellent moyen qui coûte un peu de peine et d'argent, mais est très sûr.

Si vous êtes arrêtés, n'oubliez pas que c'est un devoir d'honneur de ne pas parler. N'inventez pas d'histoire, niez, demandez un avocat.

Se taire devant la police est un devoir. C'est aussi votre intérêt. Si vous parlez, on ne cessera de vous harceler, le policier pensera toujours que vous en savez plus. La police ne vous en saura jamais gré.

Notre cause exige du courage. Elle en mérite. Nous punirons les traîtres. Nous vaincrons.

Instructions to resistance fighters published in *Libération-Sud*, 18 May 1942.

DEFINITION DU SAUVAGE

Définir le vrai sauvage c'est dire qu'il rit quand il vous frappe e qu'il hurle quand vous le frappez. Cette extraordinaire inégalité de jugement se retrouve dans tous les actes et dans toutes les paroles qui viennent de Berlin.

G. K. CHESTERTON.

Liste Noire N° 8

Nous signalons:

Jean GUYON-CESBRON, journaliste accrédité à Vichy, correspondant de la Suisse et de l'agence Transocéan, domicilié à l'hôtel Rivoli à Vichy. Agent de la Gestapo GUYON-CESBRON est à l'origine de nombreuses arrestations opérées à Vichy par les Allemands.

Louis DESPLANCHES, voyageur de commerce, demeurant 7, rue du Petit-Tour à Limoges, mouchard au service de la Gestapo.

ALLAMEL, 23, avenue du Maréchal-Foch à Marseille et POIGNAND, 142, avenue du Maréchal-Pétain à Marignane, agents du service secret de la L.V.F.

MARBEUF, pharmacien à la Baulle, fondateur du groupe local de collaboration.

CHENAUD, officier de marine, résidant à Arles, qui a dénoncé une dizaine d'hommes appartenant au maquis du Colombier.

ESCOFFIER, de la gendarmerie d'Aiguebelle, qui a assassiné un patriote.

GERBELAT, menuisier à Chandrioux en Savoie, qui a fait prendre 17 jeunes gens du maquis.

Black list published in *Libération-Sud*, 12 October 1943.

22719-4

CARTE D'IDENTITÉ

Nom : *Baron*

Prénoms : *Philippe*

Profession : *Homme de lettres*

Nationalité : *française*

Né le *25 Juin 1903*

Blaye - Gironde

Domicile *21 rue St Malo*

Rennes

Signature du Titulaire

Ph Baron

Pièces justificatives produites ou signatures des témoins

Permis de conduire

SIGNALEMENT

Taille : *1 m 70*		Menton : *rond*	
Cheveux : *Bruns*		Nez : *aquilin*	
Barbe :		Visage : *ovale*	
Yeux : *Marrons*		Teint : *mat*	
Front : *haut*		Signes particuliers : *néant*	
Bouche : *moyenne*			

Empreintes digitales

Visa
du Commissatre
de Police,

- 5 MAI 1941

Counterfeit identity card used by Pierre Brossolette.

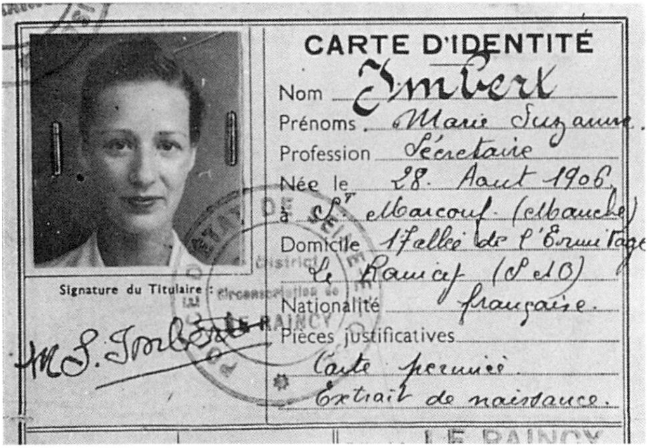

CARTE D'IDENTITÉ

Nom *Imbert*

Prénoms *Marie Suzanne*

Profession *Secrétaire*

Née le *28 Août 1906*

à *St Marcouf (Manche)*

Domicile *1 allée de l'Ermitage*

Le Raincy (S et O)

Nationalité *française*

Pièces justificatives

Carte permise

Extrait de naissance

Signature du Titulaire :

M.S. Imbert

LE RAINCY

The various faces of Marie-Madeleine Fourcade, leader of the Alliance network.

Demonstrations, Sabotage, Attacks

Maquis sabotage of the Chassezac (Lozère) viaduct, 3 August 1944.
Preceding page: Sabotage of a French locomotive requisitioned
by the Germans at Canisy (Manche), July 1944.

Sabotage of the Masléon (Haute-Vienne) bridge by the Maquis, 9 June 1944.
During the battle fought in this region on July 17th, the Maquis lost 40 men
and the Germans 342, including 7 officers.

A driverless train sent from the Mathay (Doubs) station towards the main Besançon-Belfort junction, which interrupted rail traffic for twenty-three hours in the area around Montbéliard.

Sabotage of the Grenoble-Veynes (Isère) railway line, summer 1944.

German aircraft destroyed by the Maquis at Jumeau-le-Grand (Haute-Vienne), 10 June 1944.

Sabotage of the La Butre (Côte d'Or) bridge.

The Boune army barracks in Grenoble following a Resistance raid carried out on 2 December 1943.

Sabotage at Voujeaucourt (Doubs) of a train carrying German soldiers on leave, 21 April 1944.

Demonstration protesting the S.T.O. (Compulsory Labour Service) act
at Couhé-Verac (Vienne). All participants in the demonstration were deported.
Opposite page: Funeral of Paul Koepfler, a Resistance messenger shot by Gestapo
agents at Poligny (Jura) on 31 March 1944. Defying orders from the German
authorities, a large crowd followed Koepfler's coffin.

During the night of 10-11 November 1943, members of the Lévêque
Resistance Corps installed a bust of Marianne (symbol of the French Republic)
on a pedestal in the Place Edgar Quinet at Bourg-en-Bresse.

Resistance raid in Grenoble.

Poster announcing the massacre of hostages from Châteaubriand and Nantes in reprisal for the execution, by the Resistance in Nantes, of Colonel Hotz.

AVIS

De lâches criminels, à la solde de l'Angleterre et de Moscou, ont tué, à coups de feu tirés dans le dos, le Feld-kommandant de Nantes (Loire-Inf.), au matin du 20 Octobre 1941. Jusqu'ici les assassins n'ont pas été arrêtés.

En expiation de ce crime, j'ai ordonné préalablement de faire fusiller 50 otages.

Etant donné la gravité du crime, 50 autres otages seront fusillés au cas où les coupables ne seraient pas arrêtés d'ici le 23 Octobre 1941 à minuit.

Funeral procession for Colonel Hotz, head of the Nantes Kommandantur, executed by the Resistance.

Maquisards gain control of Oyonnax (Ain) for a few hours, 11 November 1943.

German propaganda poster for S.T.O. (Compulsory Labour Service), 1943.

Anti-S.T.O. (Compulsory Labour Service) headline in *Libération-Sud*, 1 March 1943. Compulsory Labour Service was implemented in 1943 by the Vichy government on orders from the Germans, who were unable to mobilize a sufficient number of volunteers. The S.T.O. act impelled thousands of young men to "*prendre le maquis*" (take to the hills), rather than be sent to Germany. *Following page*: Demonstrations at Romans (Drôme) against the departure of forced labourers for Germany, 10 March 1943. The French police were called in to clear the tracks.

Poster announcing the death of French Secretary of State for Information
Philippe Henriot, executed by the Resistance on 28 June 1944.
Preceding page: Departure of a fresh contingent of the Legion
of French Volunteers, Gare de l'Est (Paris), 27 June 1944. Note the presence,
on the eve of his death, of Philippe Henriot.

Above: Headline in *Le Matin*, 29 June 1944.
Below: Funeral rites for Philippe Henriot.

The Maquis

Captain of the "Compagnie du 18 Juin" speaking to his men on the Place de l'Eglise, Montrachet (Haute-Loire).

The E.T.P. Francis group and their front-wheel drive Citroën.

F.F.I. truck, August 1944 (Haut-Beaujolais Maquis)

Weapons maintenance (Haut-Beaujolais Maquis).

Combat practice (Haut-Beaujolais Maquis).

Members of the Maquis washing up under the protection of an armed guard (Haut-Beaujolais Maquis).

German prisoners captured by the Maquis.

Maquis firing-line (Vercors Maquis).

Young maquisards receiving instruction in weapons-handling (Haute-Loire).

Above: Combat training (Haut-Beaujolais Maquis).
Below: Fred Telzer, Austrian member of the Lavercq Maquis,
during the Plan du Var fighting.

Two members of the Armée Secrète listening to messages and news
over the wireless at a farm owned by resistance sympathizers.

Lieutenant Roland, leader of the Morillon (Haute-Saône) Maquis,
disguised as a priest.

Burial of Commandant Hardy, leader of the Armée Secrète
in the Die (Drôme) region, who was massacred
by the Germans during the July 1944 Vercors clean-up operations.
Opposite page: Maquisards honour the spot where two Resistance
messengers were killed.

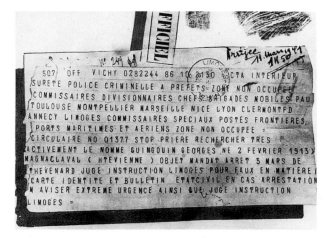

Colonel-to-be Guingouin was sought by the authorities
throughout France and at all border points.

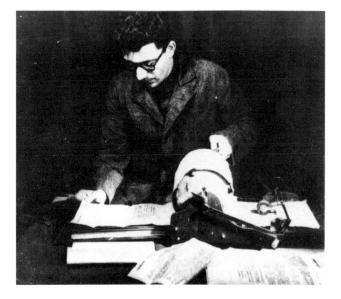

Georges Guingouin, leader of the Limousin Maquis,
using the group's mimeograph machine.

"Mama would have a fit if she could see me now!"
Cartoon by a member of the Les Glières Maquis.
Opposite page: Raising the flag, Les Glières (Haute-Savoie)
Maquis, March 1944.

HABITANTS
DE LA Hte-SAVOIE !

La recrudescence des attentats terroristes dans votre département, l'insécurité de plus en plus grande qui y règne, ont amené le Gouvernement à envisager son épuration et sa pacification.

Des mesures sévères vont être prises. Les premières de ces mesures ont fait l'objet de mon Arrêté du 28 Janvier 1944. Elles ne doivent toutefois pas être un sujet de crainte pour les citoyens loyaux désireux de revoir le Pays qu'ils aiment à juste titre, retrouver le calme et la tranquillité qui lui sont indispensables pour travailler à son relèvement.

Chargé de la direction des opérations qui, je l'espère, ramèneront la paix plus que jamais nécessaire entre Français, je vous assure que seules les Forces françaises du Maintien de l'Ordre participeront tant à l'exécution des mesures néces...ir qu'aux opérations proprement dites

Je compte sur l'exacte compréhension de tous.

Que ceux qui ne veulent pas voir répandre inutilement du sang français, trop souvent déjà versé en Hte-Savoie, écoutent la voix du cœur et de la raison. Pour ceux-là, il n'est pas trop tard pour rentrer dans le droit chemin.

Je rappelle que tout individu PRIS LES ARMES A LA MAIN, ou DETENTEUR D'ARMES ou D'EXPLOSIFS, sera immédiatement traduit devant la COUR MARTIALE : jugement sans appel et exécutoire dans les 24 heures.

Lors de l'occupation ou des engagements possibles dans les localités, les habitants sont informés qu'ils doivent rester dans leurs maisons, portes et fenêtres closes, et SE TENIR PRÊTS A REPONDRE A TOUTE SOMMATION OU REQUISITION.

Toute attitude hostile, le recel d'individus "hors-la-loi" SERONT REPRIMES SEVEREMENT, tant dans les personnes que dans les biens.

Fait à ANNECY, le 31 Janvier 1944.

L'Intendant de Police,
Directeur des Opérations de Maintien de l'ordre
en Haute-Savoie,

G. LELONG.

Poster with a message by Colonel Lelong stating that he will use French forces to restore order in the Haute-Savoie, although in fact he was supported by the Germans.
Preceding page: Funeral for a member (Tom-Morel?) of the Les Glières Maquis.

Officers of the Force for the Maintenance of Public Order in the Haute-Savoie.
Commanding officer Colonel Lelong is shown (*seated*) in the centre.

Lieutenant Morel, known as "Tom," leader of the Les Glières Maquis, killed in March 1944.

German soldiers staring at the corpse of a Resistance fighter killed in Les Glières.

**FORCES FRANÇAISES
DE L'INTÉRIEUR**

le 23 juillet 14h.15

VERCORS

Etat-Major

[handwritten letter in French]

Tenons depuis 56 heures contre 3 divisions allemandes – n'avons jusqu'à présent pas perdu un pouce de terrain – Troupes se battent courageusement. mais désespérément, car elles sont épuisées physiquement et n'ont presque plus de munitions – stop. Malgré nos demandes réitérées sommes seuls et n'avons reçu aucun secours ni aide depuis le début du combat. situation peut d'un moment à l'autre devenir désespérée entraînant des malheurs effroyables sur le plateau du Vercors. – Aurons fait alors tout notre devoir – Mais nous plein de tristesse sur l'ampleur des responsabilités prises par ceux qui délibérément et de loin nous ont engagés dans une semblable aventure.

Hervieux

A desperate plea for help written by François Huet (known as "Hervieux"),
military commander of the Vercors Resistance operation,
and sent to Algiers on 23 July 1944.

Holding out for 54 hours against 9 German divisions – up to now, haven't lost an inch of ground – troops fight courageously but desperately as they are physically exhausted and running out of munitions – stop.

Despite our repeated requests, we are alone and haven't received any help since the beginning of the battle – situation could become desperate any minute leading to appalling affliction on the Vercors plateau – would at least have done our duty to the end – but would be filled with sadness at the thought of the burden of responsibility weighing down those who deliberately and from afar, led us into such adventure.

Hervieux

Repression

BEKANNTMACHUNG

Nach eingehender Beobachtung des Verhaltens der französischen Bevölkerung im besetzten Gebiet habe ich festgestellt, dass der Grossteil der Bevölkerung in Ruhe seiner Arbeit nachgeht. Man lehnt die von englischer und sowjetischer Seite gegen die deutsche Besatzungstruppe angezettelten Attentate, Sabotageakte usw. ab, weil man genau weiss, dass sich die Folgen dieser Handlungen ausschliesslich auf das friedliche Leben der französischen Zivilbevölkerung auswirken.

Ich bin gewillt, der französischen Bevölkerung mitten im Kriege weiter unbedingt Ruhe und Sicherheit bei ihrer Arbeit zu gewährleisten. Da ich aber festgestellt habe, dass den Attentätern, Saboteuren und Unruhestiftern gerade von ihren engeren Familienangehörigen vor oder nach der Tat Hilfe geleistet wurde, habe ich mich entschlossen, nicht nur die Attentäter, Saboteure und Unruhestifter selbst bei Festnahme, sondern auch die Familien der namentlich bekannten aber flüchtigen Täter, falls diese sich nicht innerhalb von 10 Tagen nach der Tat bei einer deutschen oder französischen Polizeidienststelle melden, mit den schwersten Strafen zu treffen.

Ich verkünde folgende Strafen:

1.) Erschiessung aller männlichen Familienangehörigen auf- und absteigender Linie sowie der Schwager und Vettern vom 18. Lebensjahr an aufwärts.

2.) Überführung aller Frauen gleichen Verwandtschaftsgrades in Zwangsarbeit.

3.) Überführung aller Kinder der von vorstehenden Massnahmen betroffenen männlichen und weiblichen Personen bis zum 17. Lebensjahr einschliesslich in eine Erziehungsanstalt.

Ich rufe daher Jeden auf, nach seinen Möglichkeiten Attentate, Sabotage und Unruhe zu verhindern und auch den kleinsten Hinweis, der zur Ergreifung der Schuldigen führen kann, der nächsten deutschen oder französischen Polizeidienststelle zu geben.

Paris, am 10. Juli 1942.

Der Höhere SS- und Polizeiführer im Bereich des Militärbefehlshabers in Frankreich.

Terrorism implemented in the Northern Zone (July 1942).
A notice signed "Leader of The SS and the Police."

AVIS

Après avoir observé l'attitude de la population française en zone
[occ]upée, j'ai constaté que la majorité de la population continue à travail-
[ler] dans le calme. On désapprouve les attentats, les actes de sabotage,
[...] tramés par les Anglais et les Soviets et dirigés contre l'armée d'occu-
[pat]ion, et l'on sait que c'est uniquement la vie paisible de la population
[utile] française qui en subirait les conséquences.

Je suis résolu à garantir d'une façon absolue, en pleine guerre, à la
[po]pulation française la continuation de son travail dans le calme et la
[séc]urité. Mais j'ai constaté que ce sont surtout les proches parents des
[aut]eurs d'attentats, des saboteurs et des fauteurs de troubles qui les
[ont] aidés avant ou après le forfait. Je me suis donc décidé à frapper
[de]s peines les plus sévères non seulement les auteurs d'attentats, les
[sab]oteurs et les fauteurs de troubles eux-mêmes une fois arrêtés, mais
[au]ssi, en cas de fuite, aussitôt les noms des fuyards connus, les familles
[de] ces criminels, s'ils ne se présentent pas dans les dix jours après le
[for]fait à un service de police allemand ou français.

Par conséquent, j'annonce les peines suivantes :

**1) Tous les proches parents masculins en ligne
ascendante et descendante ainsi que les
beaux-frères et cousins à partir de 18 ans
seront fusillés.**

**2) Toutes les femmes du même degré de paren-
té seront condamnées aux travaux forcés.**

**3) Tous les enfants, jusqu'à 17 ans révolus, des
hommes et des femmes frappés par ces
mesures seront remis à une maison d'édu-
cation surveillée.**

Donc, je fais appel à tous pour empêcher selon leurs moyens les
[att]entats, les sabotages et le trouble et pour donner même la moindre
[in]dication utile aux autorités de la police allemande ou française afin
[d']appréhender les criminels.

Paris, le 10 juillet 1942.

**Der Höhere SS- und Polizeiführer
im Bereich des Militärbefehlshabers in Frankreich.**

Otto Abetz, Ambassador of the Third Reich in Paris, arriving at the Versailles hospital to visit Laval, wounded during the September 1941 attempt on his life.

Swearing-in ceremony, courtyard of the Hôtel des Invalides (Paris), on 1 July 1944.
Officers of The SS shown in the photograph include de Brinon (left) and Joseph Darnand,
secretary-general of the Force for the Maintenance of Public Order (right).

Rudolf Hess and Lafont, an officer of the French Gestapo.

Members of the French Militia marching past
an anti-Bolshevik exhibition in Paris, March 1942.

The Paris Gestapo, rue des Saussaies.

German soldiers searching private homes for "terrorists".

Farmers arrested by the French Militia.

The German Feldgendarmerie, armed with machine-guns,
checking a car at the corner of the rue du Quatre-Septembre
and rue Louis-le-Grand (Paris), September 1943.

Members of the Vercors resistance movement being taken
into custody by three members of the French Militia.
Following page: Anti-maquisard Garde-Mobile operation in Haute-Savoie.

Twenty-seven members of the Resistance go on trial before a military court
on 15 April 1942. Defendants were allowed to plead their case before
this German military court, but the Gestapo sentenced its victims without trial.
Opposite page, below: Convicted prisoners being led away following trial.
One of them is sticking out his tongue, a strong clue as
to the uniform worn by the photographer.
Above: Simone Schloss, liaison agent and member of the Special Organization
(one of the first to conduct armed warfare against the occupying forces).
Twenty-five of the twenty-seven defendants were condemned to death
and executed on 17 April. Simone Schloss, spared the death penalty
but condemned to life imprisonment, was subsequently decapitated
at the Cologne prison during the summer of 1943.

The trial of three young men responsible for killing a series of French collaborators (including journalist Paul Colin) opened on 6 May 1943 before the German Council of War in Brussels. As can be seen from the bruised face of the defendant in the centre, the three men were tortured horribly before being hanged – but they died without revealing any secrets.

Gestapo headquarters on the rue des Saussaies in the 8th arrondissement of Paris.
A view of cell No. 323 showing the iron torture-racks.

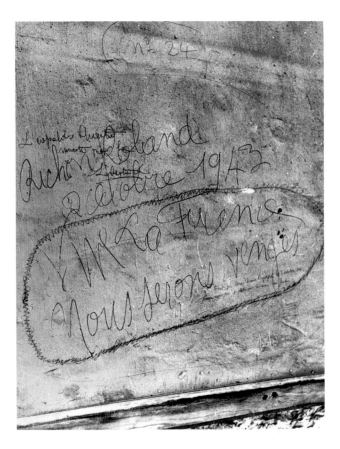

Graffiti on the walls of the Fresnes prison chapel.

Cell in a Gestapo building, Bordeaux.

Bathtub used for torturing prisoners at Gestapo headquarters
on the rue des Saussaies (Paris).

Torture implement invented by the Germans to loosen
the tongues of French patriots.

Executions,
Executed

Execution of two members of the Rochefort Resistance, November 1941.

Execution of Resistance fighters in Voiron (Isère).

Four youthful twenty-year old maquisards executed by firing squad, 18 March 1944 (Saône-et-Loire).

Resistance fighter (or hostage) being shot.

AVIS

Le 16 Septembre 1941, un lâche assassinat a été à nouveau commis sur la personne d'un soldat allemand. Par mesure de répression contre ce crime, les otages suivants ont été fusillés :

1. **PITARD**, Georges, de Paris.
   fonctionnaire, communiste

2. **HAJJE**, Antoine, de Paris.
   fonctionnaire, communiste

3. **ROLNIKAS**, Michélis, (juif), de Paris.
   propagateur d'idées communistes

4. **NAIN**, Adrien, de Paris.
   auteur de tracts communistes

5. **PEYRAT**, Roger, de Paris.
   agression contre des soldats allemands

6. **MARCHAL**, Victor, de Paris.
   agression contre des soldats allemands

7. **ANJOLVY**, René Lucien, de Paris-Gentilly.
   distributeur de tracts communistes

8. **HERPIN**, François, de Paris-Malakoff.
   chef de bande communiste, sabotage.

9. **GUIGNOIS**, Pierre, d'Ivry-sur-Seine
   détenteur de tracts communistes, détention d'armes.

10. **MASSET**, Georges, de Paris.
    détention illégale d'armes.

11. **LOUBIER**, Daniel, de Paris.
    détention illégale d'armes.

12. **PEUREUX**, Maurice, de Paris-Montreuil.
    détention illégale d'armes.

J'attire l'attention sur le fait que, en cas de récidive, un nombre beaucoup plus considérable d'otages sera fusillé.

Paris, le 20 Septembre 1941

**Der Militärbefehlshaber in Frankreich
von STÜLPNAGEL**
General der Infanterie

Notice of the terrorism implemented in the Northern Zone,
signed by General van Stülpnagel, September 1941.
Following page: Execution of Resistance fighters
on the Pic du Mont-Aigu, near Bourges (Cher).

Corpses lie in the ruins at Vassieux-en-Vercors.

At Crenay-sur-Aube, scene following the massacre
of Resistance fighters belonging to the Montcalm Maquis.

Maquisards about to be executed.

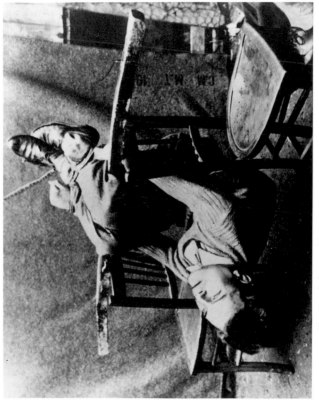

Photograph discovered in a Gestapo torture chamber, suburban Paris.

French patriot being hanged by German soldiers.

German soldiers surrounding civilians hanged at Sarlat (Dordogne) in 1944.

German soldiers and a man who has been hanged.

Citoyens de Tulle !

Quarante soldats allemands ont été assassinés de la façon la plus abominable par les bandes communistes. La population paisible a subi la terreur. Les autorités militaires ne désirent que l'ordre et la tranquillité. La population loyale de la ville le désire également. La façon affreuse et lâche avec laquelle les soldats allemands ont été tués, prouve que les éléments du communisme destructeur sont à l'œuvre. Il est fort regrettable qu'il y ait eu aussi des agents de police ou des gendarmes français qui, en abandonnant leur poste, n'ont pas suivi la consigne donnée et ont fait cause commune avec les communistes.

Pour les maquis et ceux qui les aident, il n'y a qu'une peine, le supplice de la pendaison. Ils ne connaissent pas le combat ouvert, ils n'ont pas le sentiment de l'honneur. 40 soldats allemands ont été assassinés par le maquis. 120 maquis ou leurs complices seront pendus. Leurs corps seront jetés dans le fleuve.

A l'avenir, pour chaque soldat allemand qui sera blessé, trois maquis seront pendus ; pour chaque soldat allemand qui sera assassiné, dix maquis ou un nombre égal de leurs complices seront pendus également.

J'exige la collaboration loyale de la population civile pour combattre efficacement l'ennemi commun, les bandes communistes.

Tulle, le 9 Juin 1944.

Le Général
commandant les Troupes allemandes.

In Tulle, a few days before the Normandy landings, a poster announcing the massacre of 120 hostages in a reprisal for the death of 40 Germans.

Hangings (above, in Nice; opposite, location unknown).

Der Ingenieur

JACQUES BONSERGENT

AUS PARIS

ist wegen einer Gewalttat
gegen einen deutschen
Wehrmachtangehörigen
durch das Feldkriegsgericht
zum

TODE VERURTEILT

und heute erschossen worden.

Paris, den 23 Dezember 1940.

**DER MILITÄRBEFEHLSHABER
IN FRANKREICH.**

L'Ingénieur

JACQUES BONSERGENT

DE PARIS

a été condamné à mort par
le Tribunal militaire allemand
pour

ACTE DE VIOLENCE

envers un membre
de l'Armée Allemande.

IL A ÉTÉ FUSILLÉ CE MATIN

Paris, le 23 décembre 1940.

**DER MILITÄRBEFEHLSHABER
IN FRANKREICH.**

BEKANNTMACHUNG

1. Der Kapitänleutnant **Henri Louis Honoré COMTE D'ESTIENNES D'ORVES**, französischer Staatsangehöriger, geb. am 5. Juni 1901 in Verrières,

2. der Handelsvertreter **Maurice Charles Emile BARLIER**, französischer Staatsangehöriger, geb. am 9. September 1905 in St. Dié,

3. der Kaufmann **Jan Louis-Guilleaume DOORNIK**, holländischer Staatsangehöriger, geb. am 26 Juni 1905 in Paris,

sind wegen Spionage zum Tode verurteilt und heute erschossen worden.

Paris, den 29. August 1941.

**Der Militärbefehlshaber
in Frankreich.**

AVIS

1. Le lieutenant de vaisseau **Henri Louis Honoré COMTE D'ESTIENNES D'ORVES**, Français, né le 5 juin 1901 à Verrières,

2. l'agent commercial **Maurice Charles Emile BARLIER**, Français, né le 9 septembre 1905 à St-Dié,

3. le commerçant **Jan Louis-Guilleaume DOORNIK**, Hollandais, né le 26 juin 1905 à Paris,

ont été condamnés à mort à cause d'espionnage. Ils ont été fusillés aujourd'hui.

Paris, le 29 Août 1941.

**Der Militärbefehlshaber
in Frankreich.**

Above: poster announcing the execution of Jacques Bonsergent, the man who jostled a German soldier in the street in 1940. *Below*: Poster announcing the execution of Honoré d'Estienne d'Orves and his comrades, August 1941.

Naval Lieutenant Honoré d'Estienne d'Orves, who in December 1940 led
a mission charged with locating German Kriegsmarine coastal installations
in the North of France, and who also mounted an intelligence network.
Arrested in Nantes and condemned to death by the "Grand Paris"
military court, he was executed on 29 August 1941.

Late June, 1940: Jean Moulin shown in the garden of the Eure-et-Loire préfecture
shortly after his attempted suicide, with the German Feldkommandant
who was holding him prisoner.

General Delestraint, commander of the Armée Secrète, who was arrested
by the Germans on 6 June 1943. Delestraint died in 1945
while being deported to Dachau.

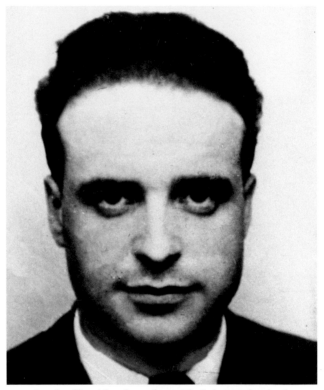

Jean Cavaillès – philosopher, professor at the Sorbonne, a founder of
the *Libération-Sud* movement, and subsequently member of the *Libération-Nord*
executive committee. Cavaillès organized the "Cahors" intelligence and combat
network. Ordered to London, he was arrested by the Vichy police just
as he was about to leave, and interned at Saint-Paul d'Eyjaux. Cavaillès managed
to escape, reach London, and continue his activities in Belgium and Holland.
He was re-arrested in August 1943, sentenced to death by the German
military court in Arras, and summarily executed.

Writer Jean Prévost, killed during the Vercors action in July 1944.

Olga Bancic, the only woman in the Manouchian group, arrested
on 6 November 1943, hideously tortured, and sentenced to death
on 21 February 1944. The death sentence was suspended for the purposes
of "additional investigation" and Bancic was transferred to Stuttgart,
re-tried, sentenced to death, and decapitated with an ax.

Danièle Casanova was born on 9 January 1909 in Ajaccio and joined
the French Communist Party in 1927. She participated in the 11 November 1940
demonstration, was active in the formation of the F.T.P. groups, and directed
a clandestine newspaper, *La Voie des Femmes*. She was arrested
on 15 February 1942 by the French Militia, handed over to the Gestapo,
and interned at La Santé prison and later at Romainville. On 21 January 1943
Casanova was deported to Auschwitz, where she died of typhus.

The Manouchian group's F.T.P.-M.O.I. (Francs Tireurs and Partisans-
Immigrant Labourers) following their arrest. At their trial they were accused
of mounting 125 armed raids, including 56 personnel attacks and 16 train
derailments. Twenty-two of the group's twenty-three members were executed
on 21 February 1944, the same day they were placed on trial.

The "Red Poster" denouncing members of the Manouchian group
as assassins in the pay of a foreign power.

15
22 *Fingercweig, Juif polonais, 22 ans, 1 attentat au pistolet, 5 déraillement*

Fingercweig, a member of the Manouchian group, executed on 21 February 1944
(German caption).

Rayman, « le tueur », Juif polonais, 20 ans, 7 attentats.

Manouchian group member Marcel Rayman, executed on 21 February 1944
(German caption).

21 février 1944, Fresnes

Ma chère Méliné, ma petite orpheline
bien aimée. Dans quelques heures je
ne serai plus de ce monde. On va être fusillé cet après midi à 15 heures. Cela m'arrive
comme un accident dans ma vie, j'y ne crois
pas, mais pourtant, je sais que je ne te
reverrai plus jamais. Que puis je t'écrire
tout est confus en moi et bien clair en
même temps. Je m'étais engagé dans l'Armée de la Libération en soldat volonta-
et je meurs à deux doigts de la victoire et du but. Bonheur à ceux qui
vont nous survivre et goûter la
douceur de la liberté et de la paix de
demain. J'en suis sûr que le peuple
français et tous les combattants de
la Liberté sauront honorer notre
mémoire dignement. Au moment de mou-
rir je proclame que je n'ai aucune haine
contre le peuple allemand et contre qui
que ce soit, chacun aura ce qu'il mé-
ritera comme châtiment et comme récom-
pense. Le peuple Allemand et tous les autres
peuples vivront en paix et en fraternité

Farewell letter written by Michel Manouchian on the eve
of his execution to his wife.

après la guerre qui ne durera plus long-
temps. Bonheur à tous ! — J'ai un regret
profond de ne t'avoir pas rendu heureuse, j'au-
rais bien voulu avoir un enfant de toi comme toi le voulais toujours. Je te prie donc
de te marier après la guerre sans faute
et avoir un enfant pour mon hommage,
et pour accomplir ma dernière volonté.
Marie-toi avec quelqu'un qui puisse te
rendre heureuse. Tous mes biens et toutes
mes affaires je lègue à toi et à ta sœur
et pour mes neveux. Après la guerre
tu pourra faire valoir ton droit de
pension de guerre en temps que ma
femme, car je meurs en soldat régulier
de l'armée française de la libération.
Avec l'aide des amis qui voudront m'
honorer, tu feras éditer mes poèmes
et mes écrits qui ne sont d'être lus.
Tu apporteras mes souvenirs à mes
si possibles, à mes parents en Arménie.
Je mourrai avec mes 20 camarades
toute à l'heure avec courage. Il sera fait
d'un homme qui a la conscience bien
tranquille, car personnellement je n'ai fait
mal à personne et si je l'ai fait, je
l'ai fait sans haine. Aujourd'hui il y a
du soleil. C'est en regardant au soleil
et à la belle nature que j'ai tant aimé
que je dirai Adieu ! à la vie et à
vous tous ma bien chère femme et
mes bien chers amis. Je pardonne à tous
ceux qui m'ont fait du mal ou qui ont
voulu me faire du mal sauf à celui qui
nous a trahis pour racheter sa peau et
ceux qui nous ont vendu. Je t'embrasse

The Liberation

COMMANDANT

Members of the F.F.I. pointing out German military positions to U.S. soldiers.
Preceding page: Liberation of the Jura, September 1944. Arrival of the F.T.P. high command.

F.F.I. group in the village of Rersaint, near Brest.

F.F.I. parade in Marseille, liberated by the U.S. Seventh Army on 29 August 1944.

The liberation of Marseille: patriots making the "V" for Victory sign under the U.S. flag.

In Nice, a jubilant population greets U.S. troops on 30 August 1944.

Liberation of Grenoble, 22 August 1944.

Liberation of Paris: General Leclerc's tank division.

Paris, 1944.

Photographic acknowledgements
Ministère des anciens combattants: 10, 19, 28, 50, 54, 55, 56, 58, 59, 64, 65, 70, 76, 77, 78, 79, 80, 81, 82, 85, 86, 88, 90, 109, 115, 117, 118, 123, 124, 125, 130, 134, 136, 147, 148, 149, 150, 151, 172 (below), 173, 175, 176, 177, 179, 181, 182, 183, 192, 193, 194, 195, 196 / Roger Viollet: 14, 42, 43, 89, 98, 92 (below and above), 132, 133, 140, 141, 142, 156, 157, 159, 160, 163, 164, 166, 167, 168, 170, 178 / Bibliothèque nationale de France: 44, 57, 66, 67, 68, 69, 74, 93, 190, 191 / Centre de documentation juive contemporaine: 46, 47, 184, 185 / Documentation française: 20, 87, 92, 94, 110, 171 / Edimedia: 17, 96, 135, 144 (below and above), 145, 154, 158 (below and above), 172 (above) / Centre d'histoire de la Résistance et de la déportation: 104, 105, 106, 107, 108, 111 (above) / Musée de la Résistance, Besançon (distribution Keystone): 83, 84, 102, 103, 112, 113, 188 / Archives Humanité (distribution Keystone): 114 / Centre Moulin (distribution Keystone): 174 / ADP-Keystone: 180 (below and above) / Robert Doisneau - Rapho: 45, 48, 49, 60, 61, 62, 63, 197 / Archives Tallandier: 71, 116, 122, 138, 139, 146, 165, 169 / Yves Manciet: 111 (below) / J.-P. Périllat: 119, 120 / Collection J. La Picirella – musée de la Résistance en Vercors: 126, 162.

POCKET 🟣 ARCHIVES
HAZAN